LET'S EXPLORE CORAL REEFS

BABY PROFESSOR

EDUCATION KIDS

Coral reefs are often called the "rainforests of the sea".

A coral reef is a community of living organisms. It is composed of plants, fishes, and many other sea creatures.

Coral reefs are the most
diverse ecosystems
in the world, housing
about 25% of all marine
life on the planet.

Coral reefs are built
from stony corals, which
in turn consist of tiny
invertebrate animals
called "polyps" that cluster
in groups.

Each polyp is linked by a living tissue to form a community. The top layer of a coral reef contains living polyps.

Corals excrete hard calcium carbonate exoskeletons which support and protect the coral polyps.

The coral reefs grow best
in warm, shallow, sunny
and moving water because
the algae that live with
them need sunlight for
photosynthesis.

Coral reefs take a very long time to grow. They grow at a rate from 0.3 cm to 10 cm per year.

The coral reefs we see today have been growing over the past 5 000 to 10 000 years.

Coral reef are naturally colorful because of the algae. If the coral reef appears white, this means there is a pollution problem.

Although many types of animals live within the coral beef, it has much more diversity in its plant life.

Coral reefs are an
important location for
finding food, shelter, mates
and places to reproduce.

The numerous types of seaweed, plankton and algae type growths that thrive on a coral reef provide food for an amazing amount of fish.

Reefs also act as nurseries
for large fish species,
keeping them safe until
they are large enough to
go into the deeper ocean.